Reading Tree

Story Sparks Handbook

Series Advisor: **Nikki Gamble**

Written by: Pam Dowson, Nikki Gamble and Ginny Germaney

Contents

Variety fiction: why is variety so important?	2
Comprehension: why is good quality comprehension so important?	3
Strategies to develop reading comprehension	6
Guided and independent reading	14
Teaching sequence	15
Building strong relationships with parents and carers	16
A closer look at the storybooks	19
The *Story Sparks* components	20
Meet the authors and illustrators	22
Photocopiable activity sheets for every book	24

Variety fiction: why is variety so important?

Throughout the primary years, children start to form their reading preferences. In order to do that they need opportunities to explore a wide variety of texts, including the full range of fictional genres. Experienced readers, who have already established likes and dislikes, should try to avoid presenting texts that solely reflect their own tastes. Of course it is also important that adults share their own reading interests, as this helps to develop a social context for reading and models the importance of making choices, which is an essential aspect of reading for pleasure.

One of the reasons that variety is important is that it allows readers to experience the full range of emotions. Humour, which is often undervalued by adults, is frequently cited in surveys as coming top in children's reading choices. Humour can help children deal with issues that might be too difficult without a lighter touch, such as loneliness, bullying, sibling rivalry, etc. Other types of humour introduce children to word play and stories like Dr Seuss' *The Cat in the Hat* invite playful experimentation and push the boundaries of the imagination.

Providing variety in fiction allows children to experience other emotions in a safe way. Sad stories evoke empathy, which is vital for developing individuals who are able to understand how others think and feel.

Spooky and scary stories allow children to explore their own limits. Some readers will be thrilled by a frisson of fear – the delicious *goosebumps* moments.

Adventure stories can provide empowering models in which children are depicted as independent problem solvers who can overcome jeopardy by using their wits and skills.

Children respond to emotional authenticity. They quickly see through an adventure that has no real peril or a spooky story that is too bland to thrill. In the formative years, however, it is important to provide endings that are reassuring and hopeful.

Story Sparks is based on these principles. The series aims to provide choice to support children's developing preferences, provide the full range of emotional experience and introduce a broad range of genres which will support children's writing.

Comprehension: why is good quality comprehension so important?

Comprehension: making meaning

Comprehension is the sense that we make of a text when we read it. Some classroom practice might lead us to the conclusion that comprehension is the ability to answer questions about a text, because this is most frequently the method used for testing comprehension.

As a result, there is a tendency to overuse questioning as the main strategy for 'teaching comprehension'. In fact, comprehension cannot be taught. Instead, an understanding of comprehension processes enables teachers to develop strategies and activities that promote the component skills that lead to comprehension.

The component skills of comprehension

So, what do we know about the processes and component skills of comprehension? As experienced readers, most of us are unaware of the skills we use when we read; although, we might become more aware if we are reading a particularly tricky text or one with a high level of technical or scientific vocabulary. In contrast, the inexperienced reader will encounter far more instances where they need to consciously stop to check their understanding. They may, for instance, encounter unfamiliar words, or be presented with an unusual sentence construction that interrupts the flow of their reading.

Over the page, the component skills of comprehension are explained in more detail. The activity sheets in this handbook have been designed to support the development of these skills and on pages 7–13, a rationale is provided for each type of activity sheet, as well as an explanation of how best to use them for the most effective learning to take place.

Vocabulary

The first thing we need to be able to do in order to comprehend a text is to work out what the words on a page mean. This may seem to be obvious and straightforward, but there are a number of things that complicate the process. To begin, young readers may encounter words that are not part of their spoken vocabulary. In non-fiction texts, technical vocabulary may be needed to explain a concept or process. In narrative texts, archaic language may be used, e.g. 'beloved'. But it is not only unfamiliar words that can complicate the comprehension process.

Bromley (2007)[1] identifies that 70% of English words have more than one meaning and these words are often apparently simple and straightforward. Take for example the word 'wild', which can mean unkempt, savage, uncultivated, natural. In some contexts the word can evoke almost opposite meanings, as in *Wildman*, a short story by Kevin Crossley-Holland, where the reader's response to the main character is determined by whether they interpret his character as wild and savage, or wild and in sympathy with his natural environment. Robust vocabulary instruction needs to extend beyond looking up 'difficult' words in a dictionary, in order to enable children to understand the finer nuances in vocabulary.

Children who appreciate that word meaning is provisional and changes as we encounter words more frequently in different contexts are best placed to self-monitor when they encounter words in unfamiliar contexts. For instance, if they come across the word 'mirror' describing a sequence of movements in gymnastics, when previously they had thought a mirror was a looking glass, they will be more inclined to stop and think what it could mean, rather than failing to comprehend the text because they cannot think flexibly about the word.

Beck et al (2013)[2] explain that thinking about words in three tiers is a more useful way of categorising vocabulary to inform teaching:

Tier 1: *basic vocabulary*

Tier 2: *high frequency/multiple meaning vocabulary*

Tier 3: *low frequency/context specific vocabulary*

Sentences

As well as understanding the meanings of words, readers need to be able to understand the meanings created by word order. This can present a number of challenges. Firstly, children's spoken and written language is not always constructed in the same way. Those children who are read to from an early age are at an advantage, as they will have had the opportunity to internalize the structures of written grammar, especially for narrative texts. Children may be unfamiliar with phrasal verbs, e.g. 'the sun was *beating down* on the old man'; or with figurative uses of language, e.g. 'the road was *a ribbon of moonlight*'.

World knowledge

Reading comprehension is more than reading words on the page. Understanding is dependent upon the knowledge that the reader brings to the text. Without this knowledge, there can be no understanding. For instance, in the well-loved picture book *Tadpole's Promise* by Jeanne Willis and Tony Ross, the joke that the frog eats the butterfly can only be understood if the reader understands that the tadpole has turned into a frog and the caterpillar has turned into a butterfly. Without that knowledge, the intended response will be lost entirely.

Helping children relate texts to their world knowledge is an important part of developing reading comprehension, as is the broadening of their life experience.

---

[1] Bromley, K. (2007) Nine Things Every Teacher Should Know About Words and Vocabulary Instruction, *Journal of Adolescent and Adult Literacy*. Volume 50, pp.528 – 536.

[2] Beck, I. (2013) *Bringing Words to Life: Robust Vocabulary Instruction*. Guilford Press.

Memory

In order to make meaning from text, readers need to be able to utilize both long-term and working memory. Long-term memory stores the background knowledge that helps the reader make sense of the text. If they can recall learning about the life cycle of a tadpole, they will understand that the frog and the tadpole in *Tadpole's Promise* are one and the same.

The working memory allows us to process new information as we read. It has a limited capacity and has to integrate the new information with the information stored in the long-term memory. So, if lots of new information is presented, the working memory can quickly become overloaded and this results in a failure to comprehend the text. Skilled readers can experience this when they read unfamiliar texts. For instance, a technical article in a research journal might be heavily packed with unfamiliar vocabulary and concepts, and might require several readings before it is understood. The reader might be aware of having to slow down and pay more attention on a word by word basis.

Inference

Inference takes place when a reader fills in gaps to make meaning. This is an ever present process that occurs at all levels of reading. For instance, readers have to make inferences in order to match pronouns to nouns, or in making connections between sentences. At a more global level they may need to infer character motivations or authorial intentions.

Comprehension monitoring

Skilled readers monitor their own understanding of text. When they come across something they don't understand, they stop and question the reasons. They may decide that they haven't read the preceding section closely enough and reread in order to get a better run at the text. They may decide that they don't have the background knowledge and undertake some research that will help them. Or they may decide that they cannot use context alone to determine the meaning of an unfamiliar word.

Encouraging self-monitoring in young readers equips them to understand the goal of reading (to make meaning) and encourages them to use self-reliance in their learning.

Reflection

Discussion after reading allows children to develop reflective skills and a more analytical approach to their reading. Opportunities for reflection should avoid an overly interrogative approach that can arise if banks of pre-formulated questions are asked in quick succession. A key question or alternative discussion opener is likely to be more successful in probing children's understanding and guiding them towards deeper reflection. A reflective discussion and dialogue might focus on the different meanings a text might have, and a range of responses from different readers. It might invite them to evaluate a piece of writing. Older readers might start to analyse the author's intentions.

Other factors

Other factors that affect a reader's comprehension include their understanding of the purpose or goals of reading. Cain and Oakhill (1999)[1] illustrated how struggling readers failed to understand why they were reading. Their view that reading was solely about decoding words inhibited their progress.

Motivation is a further factor. As with other aspects of learning, a desire to learn is crucial. In relation to reading, this means not only being able to see a purpose in reading, but also being sufficiently interested in the reading material that is available.

---

[1] Cain, K., Elbro, C., Oakhil, J. (2014) *Understanding and Teaching Reading Comprehension*. Routledge.

Strategies to develop reading comprehension

The activity sheets in this handbook have been designed to help children develop the reading strategies that will help them better comprehend text. They have been derived from the components of reading comprehension outlined in the previous section. There are 72 activity sheets in total – two for each of the storybooks in the *Story Sparks* series.

A number of clear structures have been used as the basis for all the activity sheets. This is to make it worthwhile investing time in explaining the process. We suggest that each structure is modelled with the class or a group of children first. This will enable the children to develop the language and familiarity with the process that will enable them to work independently.

The importance of oral language

In the previous section it was noted that reading comprehension doesn't exist solely within the text. For a reader to have a good understanding, they need to be able to bring to mind their existing knowledge and experience. It stands to reason that the broader and deeper the knowledge that children are able to draw upon, the better chances they have for being able to understand a wider range of texts.

Knowledge is drawn from direct experience, but it is also acquired through interaction with others (Mercer 1995[1], 2000[2]). Talking with others is a key feature of classrooms that seek to develop children's comprehension. Therefore, the activity sheets in this handbook are designed to be used by pairs or small groups of children. They require children to share ideas, to explain their thinking and to listen to others. To gain maximum benefit from the activities, children will need opportunities to work together, rather than limiting the work to individual task completion.

The question generator

Experienced readers ask themselves questions as they read. This is part of the self-monitoring process. By asking ourselves questions, we are asking, *"I wonder if I have understood this properly."* These questions might be predictive, for example, *"I wonder what's going to happen next."* Or they might be questions about unfamiliar words, for example, *"Discombobulate is a new word to me, I wonder what it means."* They might be questions about character motivations or the piecing together of a narrative. It is important that children understand that it is good to be able to interrogate a text as you read.

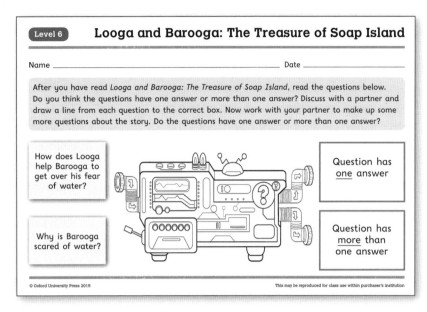

A task commonly used in the classroom is to get children to think of questions they could ask about a text. The important thing to remember when engaging the children in this type of activity is to keep the questions authentic. Ask the children to think about what they would *really* like to know and what uncertainties they have, rather than generating questions simply for the sake of asking questions.

The question generator activity sheets are designed to encourage children to ask questions about the books and then to analyse them. Two parameters have been given in these activity sheets, firstly: *Is it a question to which there is only one answer, or is there more than one answer to the question?* This activity is designed to encourage the children to distinguish between open and closed questions. And secondly: *Will I find the answer in the book, or is it unlikely that the answer to this question will be found in the book?* This activity encourages children to think about the connection between reading and the wider world. It is interesting that mature readers ask far more questions of the type that cannot be answered in the book, as they seek to connect their reading with their wider understanding.

The suggested process for using these activity sheets can be broken down into the following stages:

1. Copy the activity sheet (an A3 copy is preferable).

2. Working individually or in pairs, the children generate their own questions about the book. Suggestions have been given to get the children started.

3. Ask the children to write their questions on sticky notes or pieces of paper so they can be moved easily.

4. In pairs, the children consider how the question should pass through the generator machine. For instance, if it is a question that has only one answer, it will go in one box. If the question has more than one answer, it will go in another box.

5. The children should save this work as evidence of their thinking. It could be photographed as a record.

6. Ask the children to try to answer their own questions. They could then swap with another pair and see whether their questions were the same or different. Can they answer the questions created by the other pair?

---

[1] Mercer, N. (1995) *The Guided Construction of Knowledge.* Clevedon: Multilingual Matters

[2] Mercer, N. (2000) *Words and Minds: how we use language to think together.* London: Routledge

Statement cards

Posing direct questions is one way of engaging children in discussion about text, but it is not necessarily the best starting point. Too much questioning, especially when using a list of predetermined questions, can inhibit rather than support comprehension. It can interfere with children's self-monitoring and move the conversation away from what children need to explore in order to develop their understanding. Furthermore, firing a list of questions in rapid succession can feel interrogative and disengage children. Of course, thoughtful questioning, especially the identification of key questions and supplementary comments and questions that follow children's thinking, is important.

However, there are other strategies that can be used to initiate discussion. Posing statements and inviting children to discuss whether they agree or disagree generates a different type of dialogue. When a statement is presented, children do not have to second guess what they think the correct answer might be. Instead they have to consider and justify their thinking. The statement activity sheets in this handbook give children the opportunity to practise this type of discourse.

| Level 6 | How the Bink Got Its Stink |

Name _____ Date _____

After reading *How the Bink Got Its Stink*, read the statements below. Discuss each of the statements with your partner and decide whether you agree or disagree with each one. Then cut out the cards and organize them into an Agree and a Disagree pile. Share your ideas with another pair.

I would rather be a Bink than a Snappy Fang	To survive you need to be able to protect yourself
Fighting is the best way to protect yourself	Being clever is the best way to protect yourself
I would rather be a Snappy Fang than a Bink	Snappy Fangs eat Binks because they are hungry

© Oxford University Press 2015 This may be reproduced for class use within purchaser's institution

The suggested process for using these activity sheets can be broken down into the following stages:

1. The first time you use this structure, model the process. Write a statement on the board and explain to the children that they can either agree or disagree with the statement – check they understand what this means. Ask the children who agree with the statement to stand on one side of the room and the children who disagree with the statement on the other side, facing each other. Choose three children from each side to give a reason why they either agree or disagree with the statement. Now ask whether anyone has changed their mind. If they agreed but now disagree, ask them to cross to the other side of the room and explain why they changed their mind. Summarize by making the point that you can agree or disagree with statements and that it is important to justify your decision. Ensure the children understand that it is OK to change their mind.

2. When the children are familiar with and understand the terms *statement*, *agree*, *disagree*, *reasons* or *justify*, they can use the statement cards independently. Some of the statements that have been included in the activity sheets invite the children to relate the story to their own experience. There are no right or wrong answers to these personal questions but the children should still be encouraged to provide reasons for their answers.

3. Copy the statement activity sheets and distribute them.

4. Ask the children to work in pairs to discuss whether they agree or disagree with the statements. They can cut the statements out and organize them into two groups to show which they agree with and which they disagree with.

5. Ask two pairs to join up and discuss whether they organized the statements into the same groups. If there are any differences, ask them to explain their thinking.

6. If you want the children to practise writing their answers succinctly, ask them to select one statement they agreed with and one they disagreed with. Model how to write an answer.

Theme cards

Identifying and responding to the themes in a story is a reflective process. Themes are the big ideas that run through the story. There is an element of personal response in identifying themes. For instance, one reader might think that the main theme of *The Rainbow Fish* by Marcus Pfister is the importance of sharing with your friends, but another might think the theme is that friendship can be bought. Both of these interpretations could be justified with examples from the text. This example shows that a reader can identify a theme which may not actually be the author's intended message.

The theme cards activity sheets invite children to talk about what *they* think are the underlying themes of the story. Some of the activity sheets invite the children to relate the themes to their own experiences and others ask them to identify themes from a given selection.

The suggested process for using these activity sheets can be broken down into the following stages:

1. Begin by modelling. Copy the activity sheets and cut out the cards. Pick one of the theme cards, for example, *Fairness*. Talk about what the word means, providing some of your own anecdotal experiences. Then invite the children to share ideas about what the word means to them. Discuss how the theme might relate to the story.

2. When the children understand the concept of *themes* and *big ideas*, they can work independently with the activity sheets.

3. Ask two pairs to join up and discuss what they thought were the most important themes in the story. If there are any differences, ask them to explain their thinking.

Thinking talk clouds

The thinking talk cloud activity sheets are designed to encourage children to think about what the story tells them in the narrative or shows them in the illustration, and to use this information to interpret what a character might be saying or thinking. This requires the children to make inferences. This same structure is also used in the activity sheets to encourage children to consider what might happen next in the story or how the story may change if an alternative scenario was presented. In making such predictions, children should be reminded to consider what they already know about the characters in the story and make predictions about their thoughts and actions.

To maximize the learning potential provided through these activities, the children should be given the opportunity to share their completed thought or speech bubbles and talk about any differences in their interpretations.

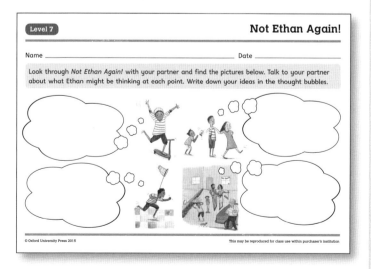

Vocabulary journal

As outlined in the previous section, vocabulary is a crucial component of comprehension. Working with Isabel Beck's three tiers of vocabulary (page 4) helps us to identify the best ways of teaching vocabulary that will enhance children's comprehension.

The vocabulary activity sheets in this handbook primarily deal with level 2 vocabulary, i.e. frequently occurring words that have more than one meaning.

Principles underpinning teaching level 2 vocabulary include raising awareness that our understanding of words comes from two sources:

1. Context – our understanding of words grows each time we encounter the word. If we hear the word being used in different contexts, we become attuned to finer nuances of meaning and we also learn that the same word can potentially have more than one meaning.

2. Definitional – these are the meanings that are given in dictionaries.

Children need to be shown how to use both of these sources to work out the meanings of newly encountered words.

The vocabulary activity sheets invite children to link new vocabulary to their existing understanding of a word, as well as looking up the meaning and then relating this back to their reading. It is important to allow children the opportunity to check how the meaning affects their interpretation of the story.

Circle diagram

The circle diagrams are used to help children relate new learning to their existing knowledge. The main use of circle diagram activity sheets in this handbook is for texts that have some factual basis or cross-curricular links, for example, the Romans. The children are invited to write what they already know about a topic in the circle, and then to identify the source of that knowledge and write it in the surrounding rectangle. Completing the circle diagram before reading highlights the importance of prior knowledge, i.e. learning takes places when we relate existing knowledge to new knowledge. These connections are crucial for comprehension. The circle diagram makes this immediately visible to the children and emphasizes the importance of real world knowledge for comprehension. Children who are unclear about reading goals and see reading solely as decoding may need this to be made explicit.

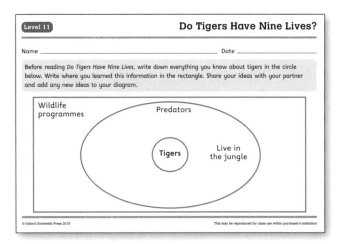

The circle diagram activity sheet can be used to show new learning during and after reading. Children can add to the diagram as they read the book, using different coloured pens to show that the notes have been added at different times.

Completed circle diagrams can be used after the children have finished reading the book, as support for their writing.

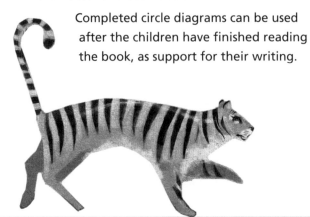

Six paragraph story

The six paragraph story is an example of cloze procedure. In order to fill in the gaps with the most appropriate words, readers have to understand the context and vocabulary in order to make an appropriate selection. For this to be an effective tool the deleted words need to be carefully selected. It is generally best to have deletions which encourage the children to think of alternatives before choosing the word that they think is the best fit. In order to do this, they have to understand the goal of the exercise, otherwise they may rush too quickly to filling in the gaps.

The suggested process for using these activity sheets can be broken down into the following stages:

1. Use an enlarged version of one of the activity sheets or a cloze procedure that you have produced yourself.

2. Introduce the text and the title. Invite the children to tell you what they think will happen in this text. Encourage them to share and discuss ideas.

3. Read the text aloud to the children, pausing at the first deletion to ask them what word comes next. Write different suggestions on the board. Ask: *Why did you choose that word?* Encourage the children to evaluate the suggestions, discuss alternatives and then think about the word that *they* think offers the best fit. The children should justify their choices using their world knowledge as well as the context and syntax of the text. Introduce the language: *predict*, *compare*, *discuss*, *justify*, *select*.

4. Once the children are familiar with the process, ask them to complete the rest of the passage in pairs.

5. Ask two pairs to join up and discuss their word choices.

Bubble maps

Bubble maps are a visual tool which help readers to describe. The object being described is placed in the centre and the qualities of the object are described in each of the outer circles. Bubble maps are useful for helping children increase their powers of description. Once children have completed their bubble maps, encourage them to use the words or images in the outer circles to describe the object in the centre to their partner. Children can use their completed bubble maps to support their own writing.

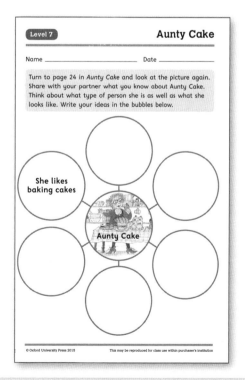

Double-bubble maps

Using double-bubble maps can help young children learn how to compare and contrast ideas. For instance, they can be used to compare two characters or two versions of the same story. Initially the language used when modelling might be 'the same' and 'different', but once children have grasped the idea the analytical language 'compare' and 'contrast' can be introduced. Two different styles of double-bubble maps have been used for the activity sheets in this handbook.

The suggested process for using these activity sheets can be broken down into the following stages:

1. Model the use of the double-bubble map. Show the children a map and draw attention to the shape. Point out the central bubbles and the labels inside them. For instance, if you are comparing two characters, the names of the two characters should appear in these central bubbles. Begin by asking the children to suggest how the characters are the same. Write the ideas in the bubbles and draw lines to connect these bubbles to both diagrams. Now focus on one of the characters and ask how this character is different from the other one. Write suggestions in the appropriate bubbles. Repeat for the second character.

The activity should be completed in the same way for the alternative style of double-bubble map, but ideas should be written either in the main bubbles or the intersecting sections.

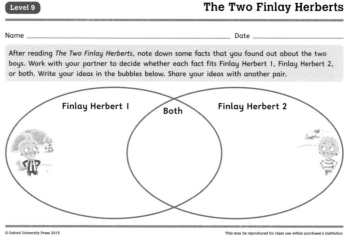

2. Once the children are familiar with this thinking tool, they will be able to use it independently. As with the other comprehension strategies, it is important that they are given opportunities to talk through their ideas with a partner, rather than working on their own to fill in the boxes.

3. A natural progression once the double-bubble maps have been completed is to use them as a scaffold for children's writing.

Story structure

Another important component of comprehension is understanding how texts are structured. For instance, a reader who has a vast experience of fairy tales is likely to have internalized basic story structures such as the 'home-away-home' structure or the 'power of three' structure. Experienced readers implicitly understand these recurring patterns and use this information to help them predict what will happen next as they read.

The story structure activity sheets draw children's attention to the key episodes in a story. Some of the activity sheets provide the key events, which can be printed, cut out and reordered to retell the story. Others require the children to identify the main events and then fill in the blank boxes. For the purpose of reading comprehension, the emphasis should be on the identification of the key events, rather than the quality of the drawing.

Research

The research activity sheets are designed to help children relate the text they are reading to real world knowledge. Making connections works in two ways: *Life to text* – readers use their knowledge and experience to make sense of what they are reading. *Text to life* – readers expand their knowledge as a result of their reading.

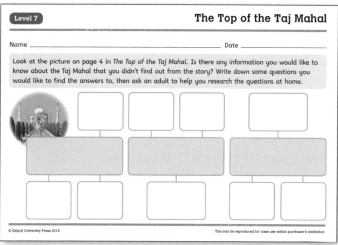

Further research can either be carried out in school or set as a homework task.

Encourage children to share their research and expand each other's knowledge before using the frame as a support for writing.

Guided and independent reading

To become skilled readers, children need opportunities to develop the skills that lead to proficiency and to practise them. Guided reading and independent reading work together to provide these opportunities.

Guided reading

Effective, well-organised guided reading sessions are immensely valuable to a child's reading development. The opportunity to share and discuss thoughts and interpretations deepens the ability to fully comprehend a text, often extending meaning far beyond that which could be achieved when a child reads alone. Structured discussion can direct attention to details that might otherwise be overlooked, thereby encouraging greater reading for understanding and enjoyment. A good guided reading session may have outcomes that exceed the expectation of planned outcomes, so it's important to exercise judgement to follow the most productive lines of enquiry and not be too constrained by a list of questions. Good opening questions are important but guided reading emphasizes the need to follow the learner's needs rather than adhere too rigidly to a script.

In the earliest stages, guided work might include a focus on the use of a range of decoding strategies, initially phonics, working towards understanding of word sounds, structures and high frequency language as a foundation. Teaching in the lower years could also highlight text structures, patterns, familiar and unfamiliar ideas, enabling children to make predictions and identify links with personal or prior reading experiences where possible.

As learning advances, the emphasis shifts towards the deepening of comprehension, encouraging the skills of summation, synthesis, comparison and evaluation. Teacher modelling of questioning, clarifying and summarising enables children to develop the skills that allow them to work independently in groups to consolidate and lead their own learning.

Essentially, guided reading is a dialogic experience – pupils explain their thinking and respond to and build on the ideas put forward by other members of the group. The teacher's role is to guide the process, ensuring the group achieve their full potential.

Independent reading

Independent reading also plays a very important role in children's reading progress. It provides the opportunity for children to practise the skills they have learnt and apply them on their own, and at their own speed. Texts should engage and excite, they should be accessible and provide challenge, avoiding the frustration that can occur when texts in the classroom do not cater for varying interests and abilities. Strategies to persevere and build reading stamina can be encouraged through teacher and peer modelling, targets and rewards.

Children like to become absorbed in what they are reading, often interpreting or building pictures as actions unfold or as characters develop. In the most conducive and motivated circumstances, they can create a kind of independent 'learning bubble', supporting both comprehension and enjoyment. This means that setting aside sufficient time for independent reading is vital. If the allotted time for reading is too short, children can complain that they were just at the point of 'getting into it' when they are asked to stop. Comfort is additionally important when reading, especially if reading for pleasure, so consideration should be given to the seating provided. Use of beanbags, soft chairs or sofas might be scheduled over time.

Teaching sequence

The books in the *Story Sparks* series have been created to engage children in reading for pleasure, and to deepen their comprehension skills. This is a suggested sequence to help you make the most of this series.

You will find detailed guidance and activity ideas in the online teaching notes: www.oxfordowl.co.uk

Group/Guided Reading

Introduce the story

Give the children some background to the story. For example, a few historical facts might be introduced to support the reading of stories that have a historical setting. Connections can be made if children have read a book from the same genre. Take the children on a picture walk of the story before reading the text. Looking at the cover, encourage the children to make predictions about what they think might happen in the story. Use statements or indirect questions such as "I wonder …" and "Tell me more about …" to develop children's ideas and engage them in discussion. Encourage them to link ideas to their own experiences. Use the online teaching notes for some specific prompts and information.

Read the storybook

Make time to check children's understanding during reading, encourage them to make predictions and engage them in discussion about characters' motives. The online teaching notes suggest places to pause in the story and talk about what's happening. Keep a balance between keeping the story moving and stopping to ensure the children have understood what is happening. As well as asking specific questions, model tentative thinking such as "I wonder what will happen next …" The inside cover notes give valuable support for reading the story in groups and for parents and carers reading with their child at home.

Return to the story

The teaching notes, and activity sheets within this handbook provide a number of prompts to help you and the children explore the plot, characters and themes and to ensure children have understood the story.

Retelling the story

Invite the children to retell the story in their own words, either in pairs or in a group. Drama strategies such as hot seating or a conscience alley can also be used to explore character actions and motivations or to improvise stories on the same theme.

Speaking and listening

Use the speaking and listening ideas in the online teaching notes and activity sheets within this handbook, for suggestions of speaking and listening activities to help support children's understanding and deepen their comprehension skills.

Writing

The activity sheets in this handbook and the online teaching notes provide a range of ideas and resources to help you create successful writing sessions linked to the stories.

Links to the wider curriculum

There are lots of opportunities to link the topics and ideas addressed in these stories to other areas of the curriculum such as Maths, Science, Geography and History. You can find a selection of cross-curricular activities in the online teaching notes.

Building strong relationships with parents and carers

Advice written by Pam Dowson, former Deputy Head Teacher

It is well known that good home-school relationships are important, and that those children with positive, informed support from home make the best progress in school.

Part of our role as teachers is to enable parents and carers to provide the right kind of help and guidance for their child, based on a mutual desire for children to achieve and be happy.

Bear in mind that not all parents and carers are confidently literate – some may have had negative experiences with school, others may not have English as their first language and so may find it difficult to help with reading and writing. You will need to tailor your approaches to suit different parents and carers.

Encourage parents and carers to share their favourite stories with their child. Emphasize to parents and carers the universal culture, appeal and importance of storytelling, giving them the opportunity to enjoy telling stories to their child, confident in the knowledge that by doing so they are supporting the work done in school.

Tips for building strong relationships with parents and carers

Here are some suggestions that you may find useful:

- Send home updates and information about reading and post them on the school website.
- Stress the importance of focusing on pleasure and understanding, as well as decoding.
- Have a fun section on the school website, with links to www.oxfordowl.co.uk, and other reading games, book-based sites and author home pages.
- Suggest related reading material to support the child's current Oxford Reading Tree book.
- At parents' evenings, display a range of books for parents and carers to browse through.
- Enlist parents and carers to help as library volunteers.
- Have one morning a week when parents, carers and preschool siblings can come in at the start of the day for a 15-minute reading together slot.
- Open the school library one evening a week after school for parents, carers and children to browse books together. Include a storytelling session, too.
- Invite parents and carers in to watch you teach reading.
- Have parents' and carers' workshops where you explain how you teach reading, how you use the Oxford Reading Tree and other books, with displays of the books for parents to see. Include a Q & A session and give them a checklist of guidelines for how to help at home.
- Send home our sample letter (page 18), making any changes necessary to fit your own situation.
- Create a display in a public area of the school – invite parents and carers to comment on their own favourite children's books and display copies of them where you can.

How to support parents and carers as they read with their child and talk about the story

When parents and carers ask "What can I do to help?" there are a number of simple, effective suggestions you can offer. You could create a user-friendly leaflet to send home, outlining these ideas, or provide just one or two each week as a bookmark, to maintain interest and involvement:

- Remind parents and carers to make reading together fun and relaxed, stopping if it becomes stressful for either of them.

- Explain to parents and carers that if their child has difficulty with a particular word while reading, they should:
   o break it down into sections and help them to sound it out
   o tell them the whole word if necessary.

- Suggest parents and carers provide opportunities for their child to reflect upon a text by giving discussion openers such as, "I wonder how … " or "Tell me about … ".

- Suggest that after reading the story, the child could be the storyteller, retelling the story. Children should be reassured that they aren't expected to remember the story word for word, but to tell it in their own way. They might even try using different voices for each character. Parents and carers could also retell the story.

- Provide customized bookmarks or reading logs for exchanging notes on individuals' reading, stressing the positive and offering brief suggestions for improvement if necessary. The child could also contribute to this conversation, perhaps with the parent or carer writing for them.

- Suggest the family joins the local library and looks out for different types of fiction. Remind them to take part in the annual Summer Reading Challenge to keep reading going through the long break.

- Stress the importance of continuing to share stories and to talk about books together, even when the child is a confident reader.

- Ensure parents and carers know how to access the eBooks, activities and advice on the *Oxford Owl* website.

- Tell parents and carers that one of the best ways to encourage children to read is to be seen reading for pleasure and interest themselves.

17

Dear parents and carers,

I hope you will enjoy sharing the *Oxford Reading Tree Story Sparks* storybooks with your child. It's so important for children to experience variety in their reading. Books should fire children's imaginations and every child should have the opportunity to read books that they are really interested in. So that you can make the most of these books, here are some suggestions you may find useful:

- As the books in this series were created to develop deeper comprehension skills, your child may initially require additional support with some elements of comprehension. Support your child's comprehension by pausing as you read to check their understanding of the story and to give them an opportunity to discuss anything they are unsure of.
- After reading, encourage your child to retell the story in their own words.
- Encourage your child to talk about the main ideas in the story and to share their own experiences and opinions.
- Look at the *Oxford Owl* website, which offers lots of ideas for how to help your child with reading: **www.oxfordowl.co.uk**
- Not all words can be sounded out – some, like 'said' or 'does', have to be learned individually, so help your child to recognize these more difficult words.
- If your child is struggling to read a word, help them to break it down into sounds, then blend them together to read the word. If they are still having problems, do it for them and get them to copy you. There's some advice on phonics on the *Oxford Owl* website.
- Encourage good expression when your child is reading aloud – demonstrate if necessary. They may not be able to do this whilst they are busy decoding, so will need to reread the sentence to provide meaning.
- When they are developing in confidence, let your child read some of their book silently, then ask them to tell you about what they have read.

Above all, enjoy the stories!

If you would like any further information or have any questions about your child's reading, please do contact me.

A closer look at the storybooks

The 36 storybooks in the *Oxford Reading Tree Story Sparks* series have been created to engage children in reading for pleasure, and to develop and deepen their comprehension skills.

Careful levelling

The books have been carefully levelled to ensure they are accessible for children at each stage of reading development.

Emotionally powerful stories

The stories in the series will make children think, laugh, get cross, feel nervous, and enjoy the anticipation of a great story!

Created to develop deeper comprehension skills

Using these stories to support and develop children's deeper comprehension skills will help children to reach the higher expectations of the new curriculum.

Something to interest every child

Including comics, rhyming stories, and picture book-style stories, there will be something in the series to engage the interests of every child.

Contemporary illustrators

34 of the best children's illustrators from around the world have been selected to illustrate the books, giving the stories all the richness and variety found in the best children's trade books.

Support for parents and carers

Each of the storybooks has notes inside the front and back covers to support adults as they read with the child. The notes include ideas for introducing and talking about the story, and pointers to help adults support their child effectively during reading.

The Story Sparks components

ORT Level	Book Band	Storybooks	Online resources www.oxfordowl.co.uk TN
6	Orange	Dear Mum; Bad, Bad Dog!; Snoot; My Sabre-tooth Pet; How the Bink Got Its Stink; Looga and Barooga: The Treasure of Soap Island	**All Level 6 titles:** TN Teaching notes
7	Turquoise	The Top of the Taj Mahal; Not Ethan Again!; Aunty Cake!; Astron; Plughole; Looga and Barooga: The Day the Sky Went Boom!	**All Level 7 titles:** TN Teaching notes
8	Purple	Doug Lugg, Boy Slug; The Story of the Train Stop; Pirate Percy's Parrot; Fisher; Charlie and the Aztecs; Superhero Bunny League Saves the World	**All Level 8 titles:** TN Teaching notes

ORT Level	Book Band	Storybooks	Online resources www.oxfordowl.co.uk TN
9	Gold	Ella's Umbrella; Sugar Plum Scary; The Football Card Coach; Grandma and the ...; The Two Finlay Herberts; Superhero Bunny League	**All Level 9 titles:** TN Teaching notes
10	White	Frankenstein's Sofa; The Greatest Viking Ever; Molly Meacher, Class 2 Teacher; Pablo's Travelling Notebook; The Dog of Truth; Agent Blue and the Super-sticky Goo	**All Level 10 titles:** TN Teaching notes
11	Lime	Stanley Manners; Rhyme Slime; Out of Control; Do Tigers Have Nine...; Julia Caesar; Agent Blue and the Swirly Whirly	**All Level 11 titles:** TN Teaching notes

Meet the authors and illustrators

A range of well-known authors and illustrators from around the world have created the *Oxford Reading Tree Story Sparks* series.

The authors

Ros Asquith

Peter Bently

Tony Bradman

Aleesah Darlison

Narinder Dhami

John Dougherty

Robin Etherington

Susan Gates

Pippa Goodhart

Sally Grindley

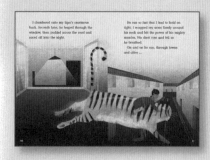

Holly Harper

Geoff Havel

Teresa Heapy

Tom Jamieson

Timothy Knapman

Sheila May Bird

Ciaran Murtagh

Joanna Nadin

Chris Powling

Sally Prue

Simon Puttock

Kate Scott

Jamie Smart

Ali Sparkes

Suzanne Torres

Fiona Undrill

Debbie White

Jeanne Willis

Jonny Zucker

The illustrators

Ros Asquith

Agnese Baruzzi

Galia Bernstein

Alicia Borges

Kelly Canby

Andrea Castellani

Rebecca Clements

Marcus Cutler

Russ Daff

Sergio De Giorgi

Olga Demidova

Jenni Desmond

Thomas Docherty

Clare Elsom

Christiane Engel

Luke Flowers

Michael Garton

Anaïs Goldemberg

Sarah Horne

Anna Hymas

Bill Ledger

Bistra Masseva

Shane McGowan

Emi Ordás

Louise Pigott

Matt Robertson

Tony Ross

Shahab Shamshirsaz

Jago

Zak Simmonds-Hurn

Jamie Smart

Jonatronix

Steve Stone

Ben Whitehouse

Series Advisor: Nikki Gamble

Nikki is the founder and Director of *Write Away* and *Just Imagine Story Centre*. Nikki has worked in education and reading promotion for over 25 years. Formerly a teacher (secondary and primary) and teacher educator, she is a lecturer, writer and education consultant. Nikki is also on the current Executive Committee of United Kingdom Literacy Association (UKLA).

Level 6

Dear Mum

Name _____ Date _____

The pictures below tell the story of *Dear Mum*. One of the boxes has been left blank. Draw your own picture in the blank box, then cut out the pictures and put them in the correct order. Use the pictures to retell the story to your partner.

Level 6 # Dear Mum

Name _____ Date _____

After reading *Dear Mum*, read the big ideas below. Talk to your partner about which of these big ideas is the most important in the story and why. Share your thoughts with another pair.

✂

Using your imagination	Travelling and visiting places
There is no place like home	Quests and adventures
Winning	Helping friends
Solving problems	Making money

Level 6

Bad, Bad Dog

Name _____ Date _____

After reading *Bad, Bad Dog*, read the statements below. Discuss each of the statements with your partner and decide whether you agree or disagree with each one. Then cut out the cards and organize them into an Agree and a Disagree pile. Discuss your ideas with another pair.

Miss Petal accidentally tripped the man carrying the apples	**You cannot judge someone by the way they look**
Big dogs are not as well behaved as small ones	**Miss Petal did not mean to behave badly**
Growly gets blamed for things that he did not do	**Miss Petal blamed Growly to cover up her bad behaviour**
Pets are like their owners	**Growly tried to tell the lady with the little boy that Miss Petal had stolen the ice cream**

Bad, Bad Dog

Level 6

Name _____ Date _____

> Use your knowledge of the story, *Bad, Bad Dog*, to work out what the missing words are. Write them in the gaps. Check your story makes sense by reading it to your partner. Have you used the same words or different ones?

Everybody said Miss Petal was a _____ old lady. And everybody said that Growly was a _____ dog.

Miss Petal and Growly went for a walk. They met a man _____ a hat, and a lady with a little boy.

Miss Petal _____ the little boy's ice cream. Then she _____ a man carrying a box of apples. The apples _____ across the road. Miss Petal _____ the apples and put them in her bag.

At the fish shop, Miss Petal tied Growly to a post. She _____ a lovely little dog. Growly tried to _____ the owner by growling.

Miss Petal was _____.

Growly went to live with Alf from the fish shop. They lived happily ever after.

Level 6

Snoot

Name _____ Date _____

At the end of the story, Snoot is much happier. Talk with your partner about how Snoot's dreams might have changed. Draw pictures in each of the bubbles to show some of the things you dream about.

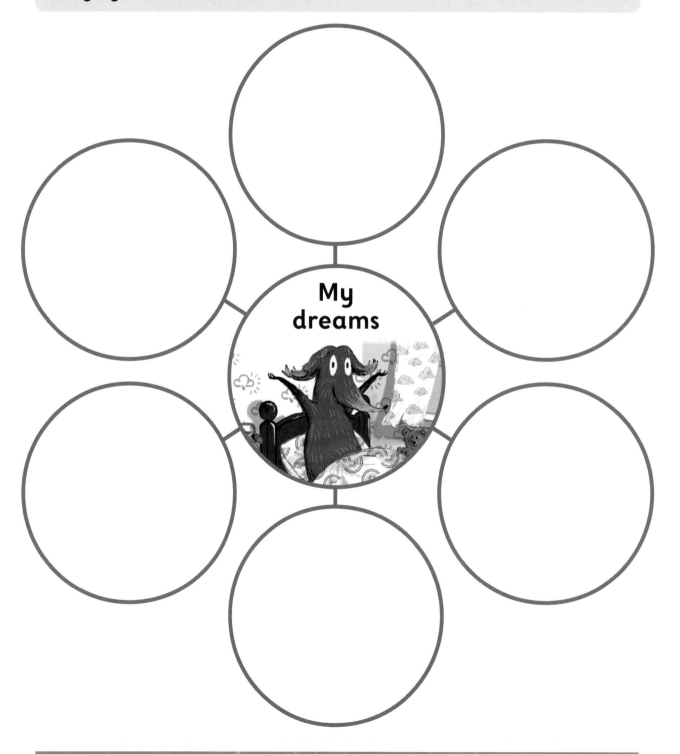

Level 6

Snoot

Name _____ Date _____

Look at the pictures below and talk to your partner about what Snoot is thinking in each picture. Write your ideas in the thought bubbles. Share your ideas with another pair.

| Level 6 | My Sabre-tooth Pet |

Name _____ Date _____

The pictures below tell the story of *My Sabre-tooth Pet*. One of the boxes has been left blank. Draw your own picture in the blank box, then cut out the pictures and put them in the correct order. Use the pictures to retell the story to your partner.

| Level 6 | # My Sabre-tooth Pet |

Name _____   Date _____

After reading *My Sabre-tooth Pet*, read the big ideas below. Talk to your partner about which of these big ideas is the most important in the story and why. Share your ideas with another pair.

✂

Taking part is more important than winning	**You can be small but mighty**
Friends are always there when you need them	**Pets make great friends**
You can be scared and brave	**Appreciate what you have**

Level 6

How the Bink Got Its Stink

Name _____ Date _____

The pictures below tell the story of *How the Bink Got Its Stink*. One of the boxes has been left blank. Draw your own picture in the blank box, then cut out the pictures and put them in the correct order. Use the pictures to retell the story to your partner.

Level 6

How the Bink Got Its Stink

Name _____ Date _____

> After reading *How the Bink Got Its Stink*, read the statements below. Discuss each of the statements with your partner and decide whether you agree or disagree with each one. Then cut out the cards and organize them into an Agree and a Disagree pile. Share your ideas with another pair.

✂

I would rather be a Bink than a Snappy Fang	**To survive you need to be able to protect yourself**
Fighting is the best way to protect yourself	**Being clever is the best way to protect yourself**
I would rather be a Snappy Fang than a Bink	**Snappy Fangs eat Binks because they are hungry**

Level 6

Looga and Barooga: The Treasure of Soap Island

Name _____ Date _____

After you have read Looga and Barooga: The Treasure of Soap Island, read the questions below. Do you think the questions have one answer or more than one answer? Discuss with a partner and draw a line from each question to the correct box. Now work with your partner to make up some more questions about the story. Do the questions have one answer or more than one answer?

How does Looga help Barooga to get over his fear of water?

Why is Barooga scared of water?

Question has one answer

Question has more than one answer

Level 6

Looga and Barooga: The Treasure of Soap Island

Name _____ Date _____

Look at page 24 in *Looga and Barooga: The Treasure of Soap Island*. Talk to your partner about what might happen next in the story. How do you think Looga could help Barooga get over his fear of the octopus and the pirates? Think about what ideas Looga might have and write them in the bubbles. Work with your partner and use your ideas to perform a role play.

Level 7

Plughole

Name _____ Date _____

At the beginning of *Plughole*, the boy is thinking about what he might find down the plughole. Do you think he would be surprised to find a monster? How do you think the monster would feel?

Level 7   **Plughole**

Name _____ Date _____

The story *Plughole* is set in an imaginary world down a plughole. Can you think of any other imaginary worlds where a story could be set? Share your ideas with your partner and add them to the bubble map.

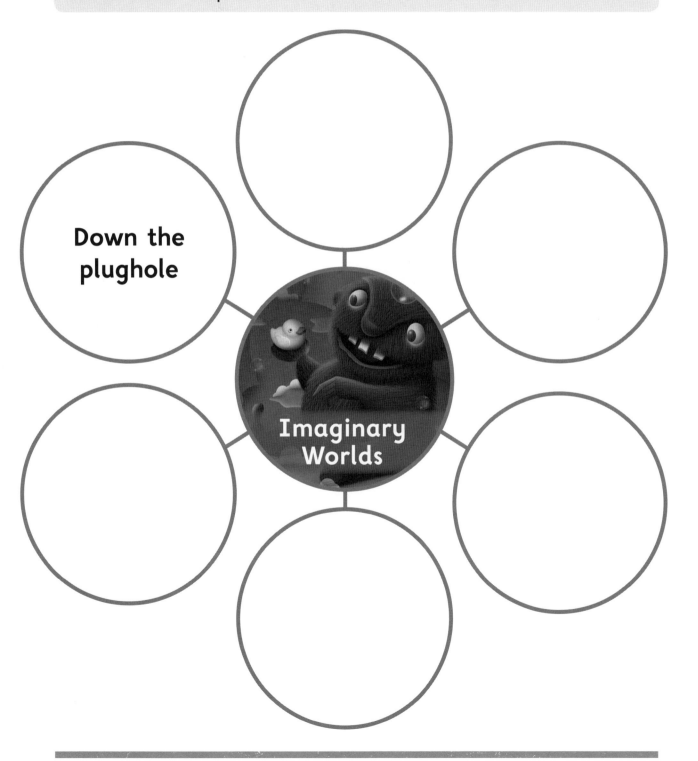

Level 7 — The Top of the Taj Mahal

Name _____ Date _____

Turn to the title page in *The Top of the Taj Mahal* and reread the information about the Taj Mahal. Share with your partner what else you found out about the Taj Mahal when reading the story. Write your ideas in the bubbles.

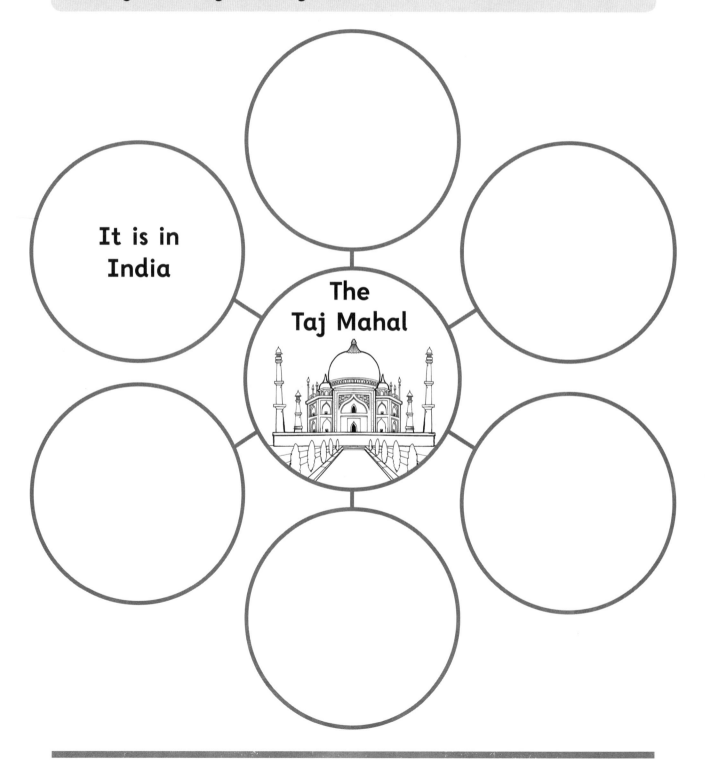

Level 7

The Top of the Taj Mahal

Name _____ Date _____

Look at the picture on page 4 in *The Top of the Taj Mahal*. Is there any information you would like to know about the Taj Mahal that you didn't find out from the story? Write down some questions you would like to find the answers to, then ask an adult to help you research the questions at home.

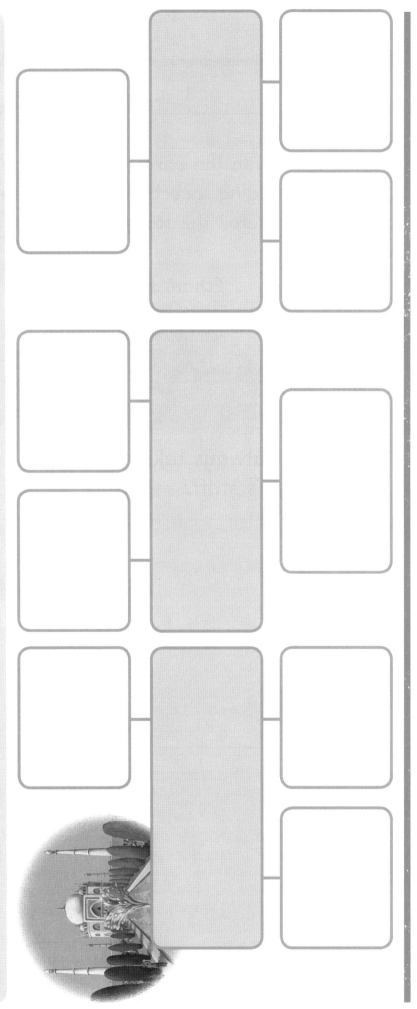

| Level 7 | Not Ethan Again! |

Name _____ Date _____

Draw pictures in the boxes below to retell the story *Not Ethan Again!* Try adding speech bubbles and captions. Use your drawings to retell the story to your partner.

"Ethan, stop!"

Ethan was always taking Jessie's stuff.

Level 7

Not Ethan Again!

Name _____ Date _____

Look through *Not Ethan Again!* with your partner and find the pictures below. Talk to your partner about what Ethan might be thinking at each point. Write down your ideas in the thought bubbles.

Level 7

Aunty Cake

Name _____ Date _____

Turn to page 24 in *Aunty Cake* and look at the picture again. Share with your partner what you know about Aunty Cake. Think about what type of person she is as well as what she looks like. Write your ideas in the bubbles below.

Aunty Cake

Level 7

Name _____ Date _____

Look at page 11 in *Aunty Cake*. Talk to your partner about what might have happened to Aunty Cake if the boy hadn't told everyone who she was. Think about what each person might have said and write your ideas in the bubbles. Work in a small group and use your speech bubbles to perform a role play.

Level 7

Astron

Name _____ Date _____

After you have read Astron, read the questions below. Do you think the answers are in the book or not in the book? Discuss with a partner and draw a line from each question to the correct box. Now work with your partner to make up some more questions about the story. Can the answers be found in the book or not?

Why are Olivia and her family travelling in space?

What are the creatures that attack the spaceship called?

Answer is in the book

Answer is not in the book

© Oxford University Press 2015

This may be reproduced for class use within purchaser's institution

44

Astron

Level 7

Name _____ Date _____

In *Astron*, Olivia and Astron come from different worlds. Discuss the two characters with your partner and identify their similarities and differences. Write your ideas in the bubbles, then share your ideas with another pair.

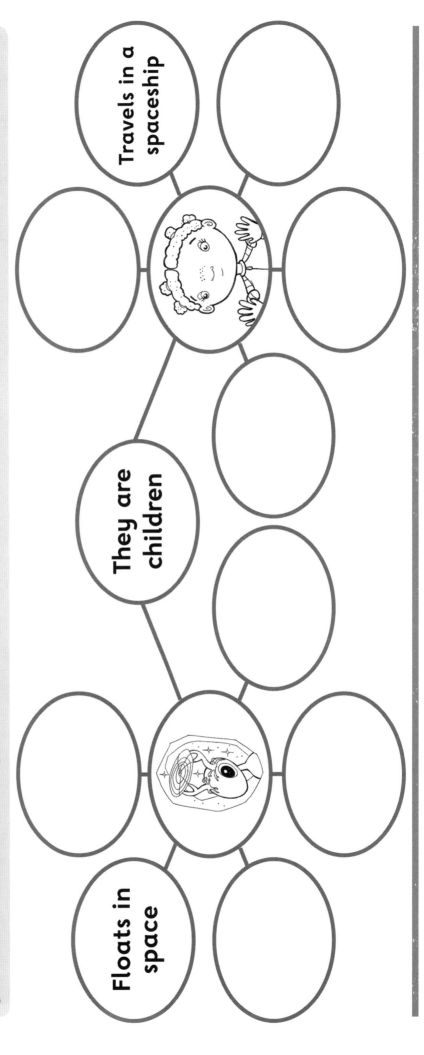

Level 7   Looga and Barooga: The Day the Sky Went Boom!

Name _____ Date _____

Turn to page 11 in *Looga and Barooga: The Day the Sky Went Boom!* Share with your partner what you found out about the giants in the story. Write your ideas in the bubbles below.

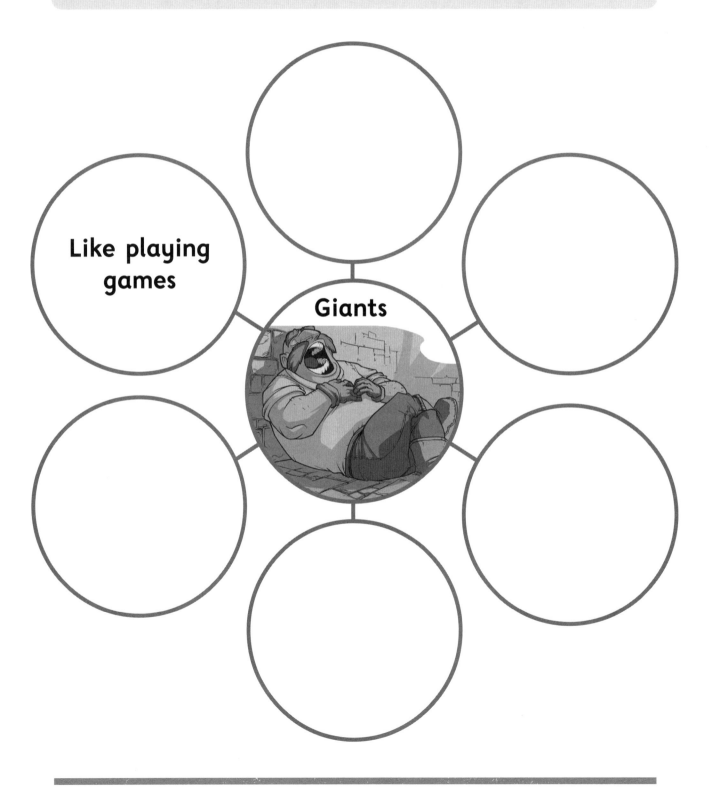

Level 7

Looga and Barooga: The Day the Sky Went Boom!

Name _____ Date _____

Is thunder made by giants? Are rainbows really used to travel between the clouds? Read through the questions below with a partner. Discuss the questions in a small group and write down any facts you already know. Ask an adult to help you research any questions you don't know the answers to at home.

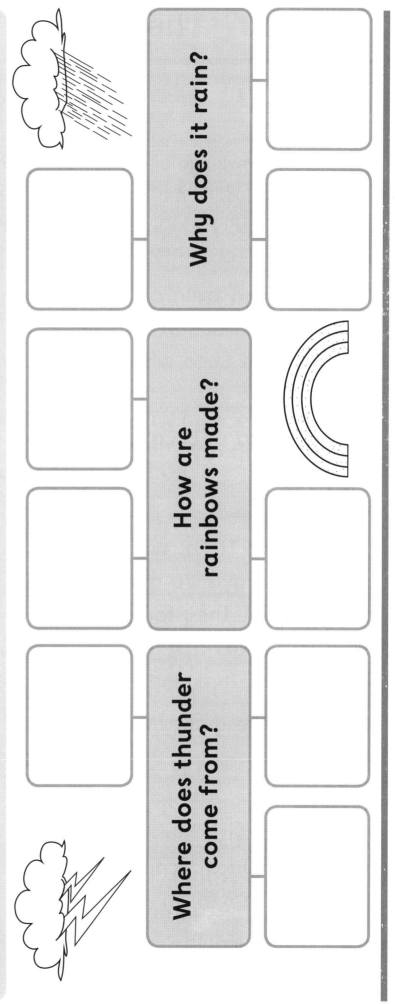

47

Level 8 — The Story of the Train Stop

Name _____ Date _____

> Use your knowledge of the story, *The Story of the Train Stop*, to work out what the missing words are. Write them in the gaps. Check your story makes sense by reading it to your partner. Have you used the same words or different ones?

Eva was on a train on the way to _____ her grandad. Eva began to _____ a story about a boy called Luca who lived in a village where it never stopped _____.

In the story, Luca and his dog, Ticket, went on an _____ to find some treasure. The treasure had been _____ by a giant.

Luca and Ticket went _____ a forest, _____ a mountain and _____ some waves. They found a _____. Inside the lighthouse was a _____.

The _____ told Luca that there was no treasure. The giant blew away the _____ and made the _____ disappear.

Luca _____ the giant to come back to the village with him. The crowds _____ and everyone had a picnic in the sunshine to _____.

At last, the train _____ at granddad's station. Eva couldn't wait to read him her _____ story.

Level 8 — The Story of the Train Stop

Name _____ Date _____

After reading *The Story of the Train Stop*, read the statements below. Discuss each of the statements with your partner and decide whether you agree or disagree with each one. Then cut out the cards and organize them into an Agree and a Disagree pile. Share your ideas with another pair.

Luca loved taking his cat on adventures	It never rains in the village where Luca and Ticket live
The giant was clever to tell people he had hidden some treasure	No one would help Eva with ideas for her story
Luca's village sold wellington boots all year round	Ticket was not afraid of the dark and creepy forest

Level 8

Pirate Percy's Parrot

Name _____ Date _____

Before reading *Pirate Percy's Parrot*, write down everything you know about pirates in the circle below. Then write where you learned this information in the rectangle. Share your ideas with your partner and add any new ideas to your diagram.

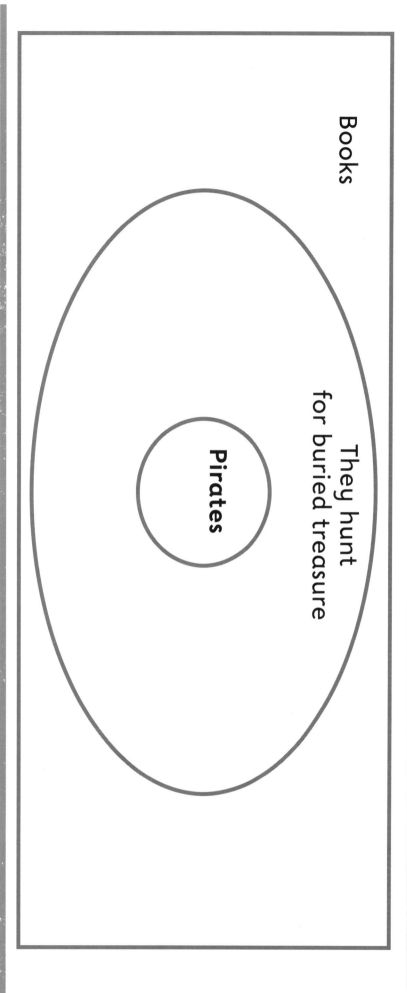

Books

They hunt for buried treasure

Pirates

Level 8 — Pirate Percy's Parrot

Name _____   Date _____

Read through the list of words with your partner. Find each of the words in *Pirate Percy's Parrot* and write down the sentence in the story where it appears. Talk with your partner about what you think each word means. Use a dictionary to check your ideas, then write down a definition.

New word	Sentence in the story	Definition
chest (page 4)		
growled (page 6)		
howling (page 8)		
bobbing (page 12)		
missed (page 16)		

Level 8

The Wish Fisher

Name _____   Date _____

After reading *The Wish Fisher*, read the big ideas below. Talk to your partner about which of these big ideas is the most important in the story and why. Share with your partner what these ideas mean to you. Have you ever been selfish, or given something up for a good reason?

Being selfish	Giving up something really important to you for the sake of someone else
Having responsibility for something	Keeping traditions

The Wish Fisher

Level 8

Name _____ Date _____

Look through *The Wish Fisher* with your partner and find the pictures below. Talk to your partner about what the Emperor and Sakura might be thinking at each point. Write down your ideas in the thought bubbles.

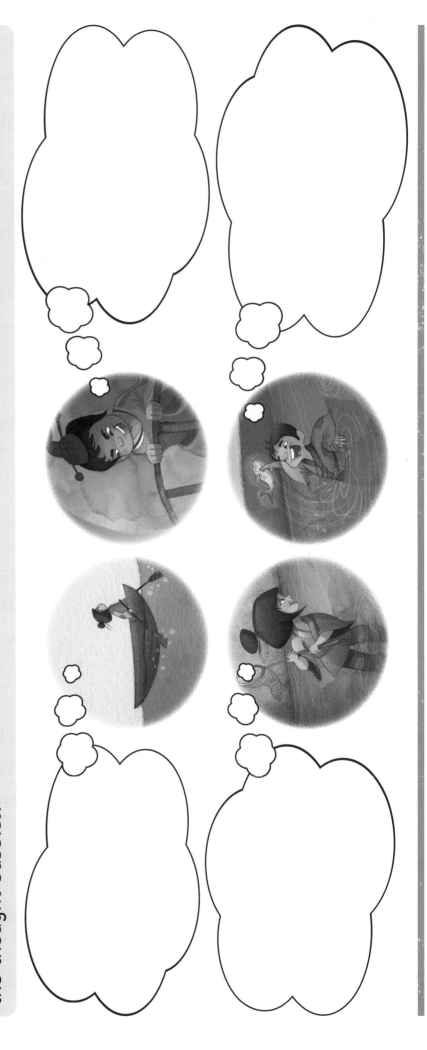

| Level 8 | **Doug Lugg, Boy Slug** |

Name _____ Date _____

After reading *Doug Lugg, Boy Slug*, read the statements below. Discuss each of the statements with your partner and decide whether you agree or disagree with each one. Then cut out the cards and organize them into an Agree and a Disagree pile. Discuss your ideas with another pair.

✂

Doug loves spinach before he turns into a slug	**It would be fun to be a slug for a night**
The slugs are frightened of Doug because he is a giant boy	**Turning into a slug made Doug love vegetables**
Slugs eat cabbage	**The security at the supermarket is not very good**
Mrs Lugg should have put the slug powder somewhere safer	**Jack was very unlucky**

Level 8

Doug Lugg, Boy Slug

Name _____ Date _____

At the end of *Doug Lugg, Boy Slug*, Mrs Lugg is surprised to find that all the slug powder has disappeared. Do you think Doug remembers what happened? Talk to your partner about what you think Doug and Mrs Lugg are thinking at this point in the story. Write your ideas in the thought bubbles.

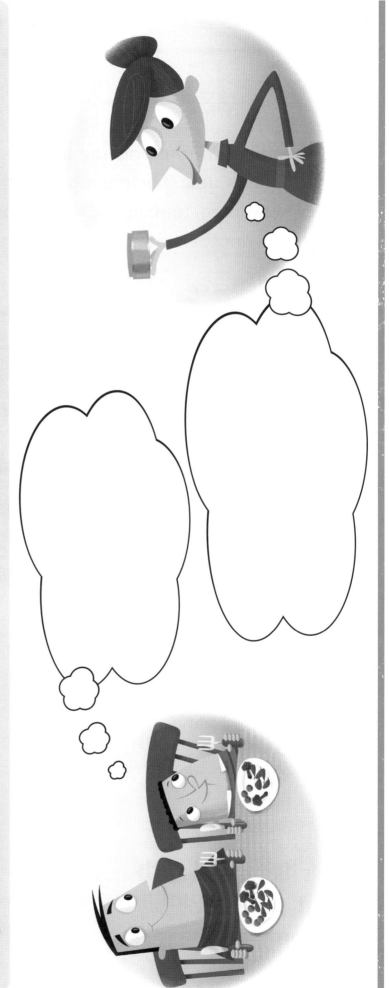

Level 8

Charlie and the Aztecs

Name _____ Date _____

After reading *Charlie and the Aztecs*, read the big ideas below. Talk to your partner about which of these big ideas is the most important in the story and why. Share your ideas with another pair.

Fairness	Time travel
Boys and girls are equal	**Wisdom**

| Level 8 | **Charlie and the Aztecs** |

Name _____ Date _____

The pictures below tell the story of *Charlie and the Aztecs*. One of the boxes has been left blank. Draw your own picture in the blank box. Cut out the pictures and put them in the correct order, then use the pictures to retell the story to your partner.

© Oxford University Press 2015 — This may be reproduced for class use within purchaser's institution

Level 8

Superhero Bunny League Saves the World!

Name _____ Date _____

Before reading *Superhero Bunny League Saves the World!*, write down everything you know about superheroes in the circle below. Write where you learned this information in the rectangle. Share your ideas with your partner and add any new ideas to your diagram.

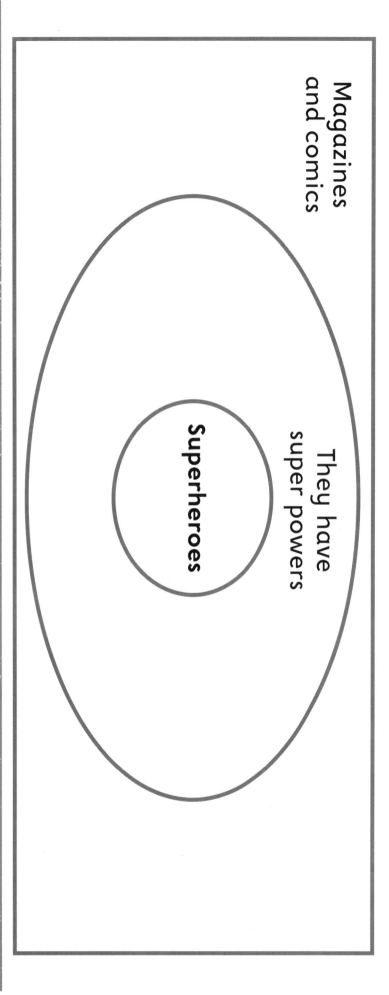

Magazines and comics

They have super powers

Superheroes

Superhero Bunny League Saves the World!

Level 8

Name _____ Date _____

Look at the pictures on page 12 of *Superhero Bunny League Saves the World!* Do all superheroes wear capes like Stumpy? What other super powers do superheroes have? Work with your partner or in a small group to discuss the answers to the questions below. Write down your ideas in the boxes. Ask an adult to help you research any questions you don't know the answers to at home.

What powers can superheroes have?

What costumes can superheroes wear?

What gadgets can superheroes have?

Level 9

Ella's Umbrella

Name _____   Date _____

In the story *Ella's Umbrella*, Ella's grandpa is an inventor. Think about the inventions you have at home and add them to the bubble map. Choose one invention and find out more about it.

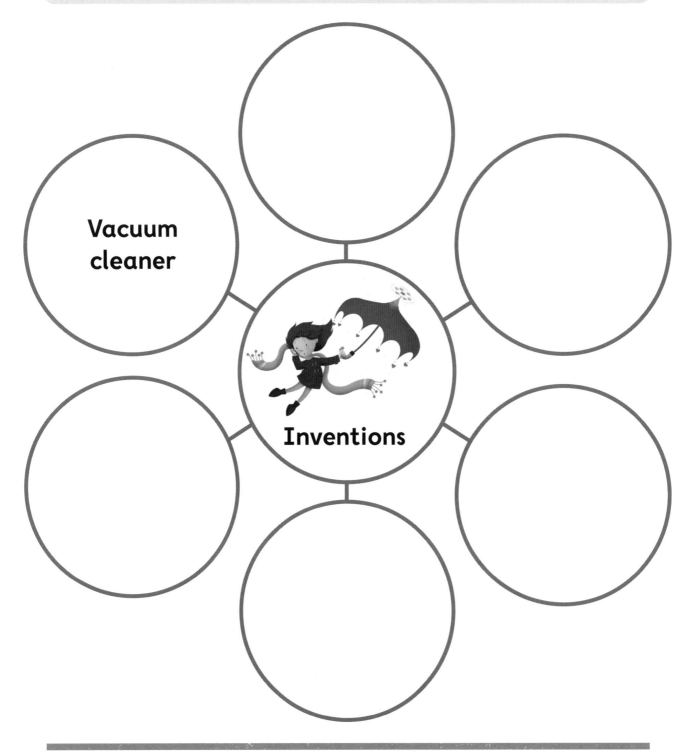

Level 9 — Ella's Umbrella

Name _____   Date _____

Read through the list of words with your partner. Find each of the words in *Ella's Umbrella*. Write down the sentence in the story where each word appears. Talk with your partner about what you think each word means. Use a dictionary to check your ideas, then write down a definition.

New word	Sentence in the story	Dictionary definition
floating (page 8)		
trouble (page 9)		
drifted (page 13)		
skimmed (page 14)		
harder (page 18)		

Sugar Plum Scary

Level 9

Name _____ Date _____

After you have read Sugar Plum Scary, read the questions below. Do you think the answers are in the book or not in the book? Discuss with a partner and draw a line from each question to the correct box. Now work with your partner to make up some more questions about the story. Can the answers be found in the book or not?

What is the name of Sugar Plum's best friend?

Why is Verruca mean to Sugar Plum?

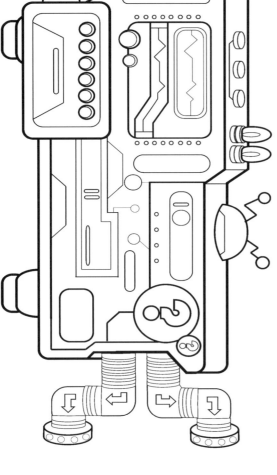

Answer **is** in the book

Answer is **not** in the book

Level 9

Sugar Plum Scary

Name _____ Date _____

Look at page 21 in *Sugar Plum Scary*. Talk to your partner about what else could have happened to the coins. What if a bad fairy was stealing the coins to get Bottletop or Sugar Plum into trouble? Discuss different ideas with your partner. Think about what each person might have said and write your ideas in the bubbles. Work in a small group and use your speech bubbles to perform a role play.

The Football Card Coach

Name _____ Date _____

After you have read *The Football Card Coach*, read the questions below. Do you think the answers are in the book or not in the book? Discuss with a partner and draw a line from each question to the correct box. Now work with your partner to make up some more questions about the story. Can the answers be found in the book or not?

Why is Kev mean to Jack?

What is the name of the player on the gold star card?

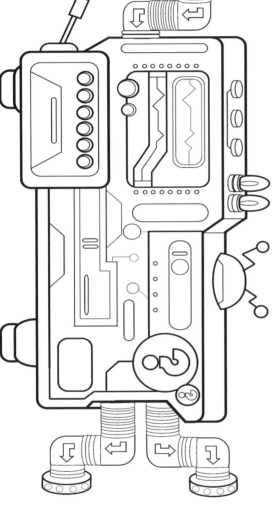

Answer is in the book

Answer is not in the book

Level 9   # The Football Card Coach

Name _____   Date _____

After reading *The Football Card Coach*, read the big ideas below. Talk to your partner about which of these big ideas is the most important in the story. Share your ideas with another pair.

Keep trying and never give up	**Practice makes perfect**
Always believe in yourself	**Friends look after each other**
Being good is always rewarded	**Follow your dreams**

Grandma and the Leopard

Level 9

Name _____ Date _____

After reading *Grandma and the Leopard*, read the statements below. Discuss each of the statements with your partner and decide whether you agree or disagree with each one. Then cut out the cards and organize them into an Agree and a Disagree pile. Discuss your ideas with another pair.

✂

You should always listen to the end of a story	Leopards are frightened of loud noises
Ava should not have told Elise Grandma's story	Your imagination can play tricks on you if you are frightened
Grandma should not have told Ava the leopard story	Sometimes it is exciting to feel a bit scared
Daytime is scarier than night-time	Big sisters should always look after their younger brothers or sisters

Level 9

Grandma and the Leopard

Name _____ Date _____

In *Grandma and the Leopard*, Elise and Ava are both frightened by Grandma's story but they deal with it in different ways. On page 22, Elise hides in the classroom cupboard. Talk to your partner about what you think Ava, Elise and the teacher are thinking at this point in the story.

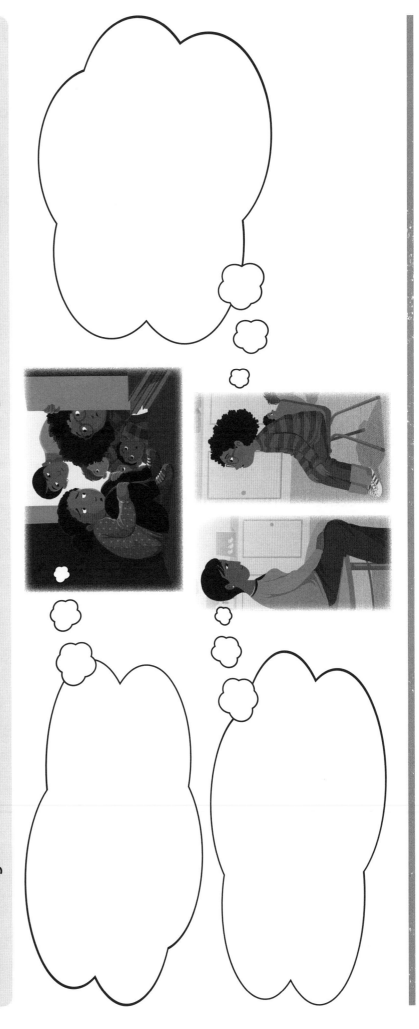

Level 9 The Two Finlay Herberts

Name _____ Date _____

Draw pictures in the boxes below to retell the story, *The Two Finlay Herberts*. Try adding speech bubbles and captions. Use your drawings to retell the story to your partner.

My name is Finlay Herbert.

There were two boys both called Finlay Herbert.

Level 9

The Two Finlay Herberts

Name _____ Date _____

After reading *The Two Finlay Herberts*, note down some facts that you found out about the two boys. Work with your partner to decide whether each fact fits Finlay Herbert 1, Finlay Herbert 2, or both. Write your ideas in the bubbles below. Share your ideas with another pair.

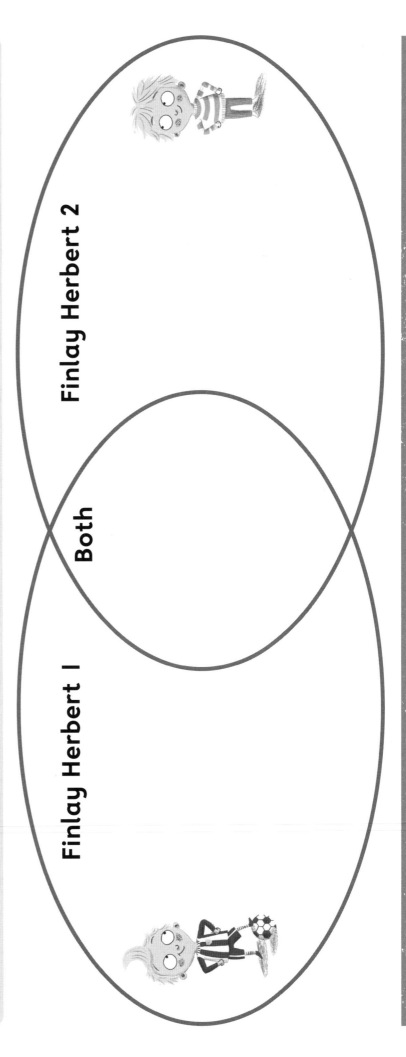

Level 9 | Superhero Bunny League in Space!

Name _____ Date _____

After reading *Superhero Bunny League in Space!*, read the big ideas below. Talk to your partner about which of these big ideas is the most important in the story and why. Share your ideas with another pair.

Teamwork	Greed
Goodie	Baddie
Friendship	Victory

Level 9

Superhero Bunny League in Space!

Name _____ Date _____

After reading *Superhero Bunny League in Space!*, note down some facts that you found out about Stumpy and Handsome Steve. Work with your partner to decide whether each fact fits Stumpy, Handsome Steve, or both. Write your ideas in the bubbles below. Share your ideas with another pair.

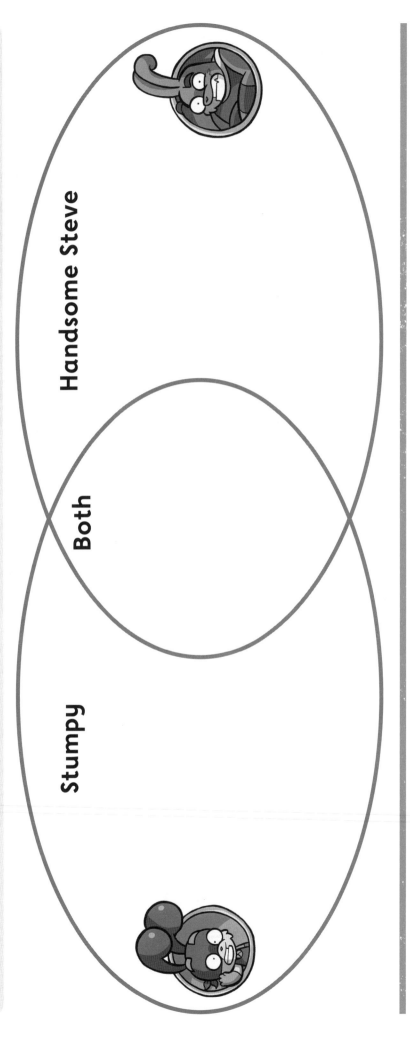

© Oxford University Press 2015

This may be reproduced for class use within purchaser's institution

Level 10

Frankenstein's Sofa

Name _____ Date _____

> Use your knowledge of the story, *Frankenstein's Sofa*, to work out what the missing words are. Check your story makes sense by reading it to your partner. Have you used the same words or different ones?

Victor Frankenstein was an _____. He tried to make scary things but his inventions were never very _____.

Every month, Victor had a _____ with his friends to see who could invent the _____ thing.

Victor decided to make a _____. He brought his _____ Lightning Catcher Machine down from the roof and set it up in his workshop.

After some time, Victor finally heard thunder and a bolt of lightning _____ through the machine. The lightning hit the _____ and it _____ to life.

Victor's friends _____ and it was Victor's turn to show his scariest thing. Suddenly, there was a _____ from upstairs.

At first, Victor was _____ of the snapping, pink sofa monster. But when it _____ his friends and won him the trophy for the scariest thing ever, he felt _____.

Frankenstein's Sofa

Level 10

Name _____ Date _____

After reading *Frankenstein's Sofa*, read the statements below. Discuss each of the statements with your partner and decide whether you agree or disagree with each one. Then cut out the cards and organize them into an Agree and a Disagree pile. Discuss your ideas with another pair.

Victor's friends were not always kind to him	All inventors live in castles
Cheese-flavoured sweets make your nose fall off	Victor was proud of his sofa-monster
Victor's grandfather kept bees at the castle	Aunty Doris loved baking cakes

The Greatest Viking Ever

Name _____ Date _____

In *The Greatest Viking Ever*, Olaf and Ivar are brothers. But are they alike? Discuss the two characters with your partner and identify their similarities and differences. Write your ideas in the bubbles. Share your ideas with another pair.

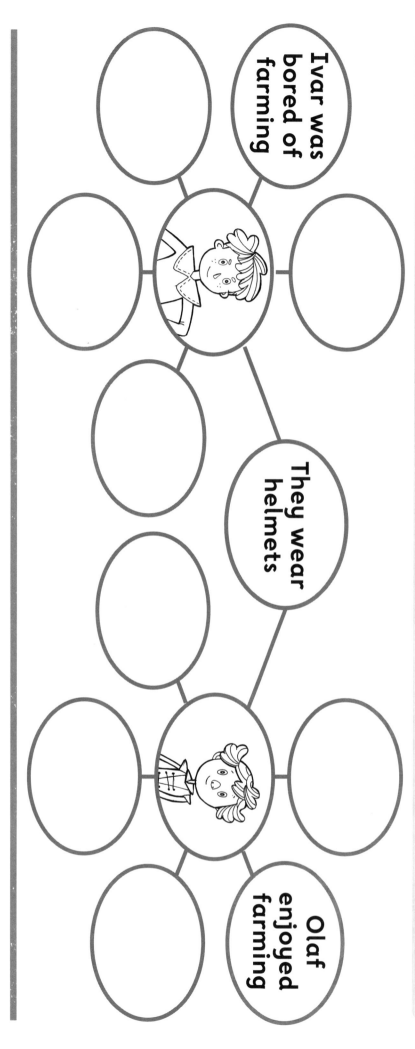

Level 10

The Greatest Viking Ever

Name _____ Date _____

At the end of *The Greatest Viking Ever*, Ivar told everyone about his great adventure. But Ivar's version of the story isn't quite as Olaf remembered it. What do you think Ivar is telling everyone? What is Olaf thinking as he listens to his brother? Write your ideas in the bubbles below, then share your ideas with your partner.

Molly Meacher, Class 2 Teacher

Name _____ Date _____

Before reading *Molly Meacher, Class 2 Teacher*, write down everything you know about baking in the circle below. Then write where you learned this information in the rectangle. Share your ideas with your partner and add any new ideas to your diagram.

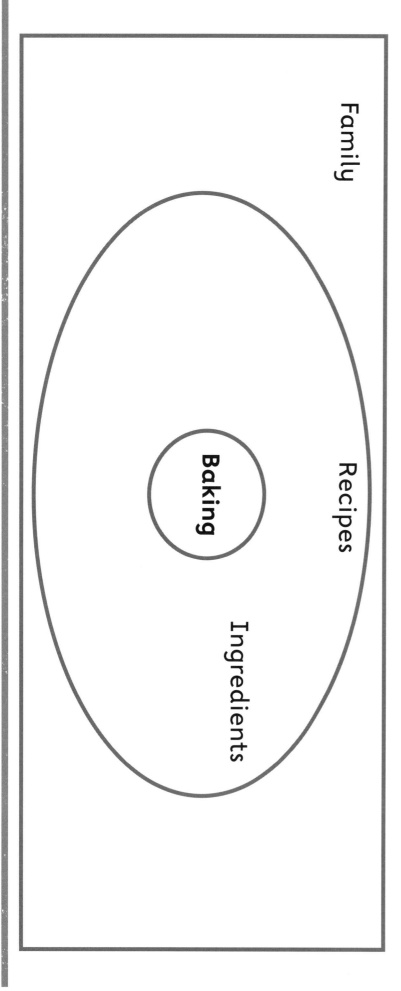

Molly Meacher, Class 2 Teacher

Level 10

Name _____ Date _____

Look at page 7 in *Molly Meacher, Class 2 Teacher*. Talk to your partner about what might have happened if there had been something different in the envelope. What if it had been money or football tickets? Think about what each person might have said and write your ideas in the bubbles. Work in a small group and use your speech bubbles to perform a role play.

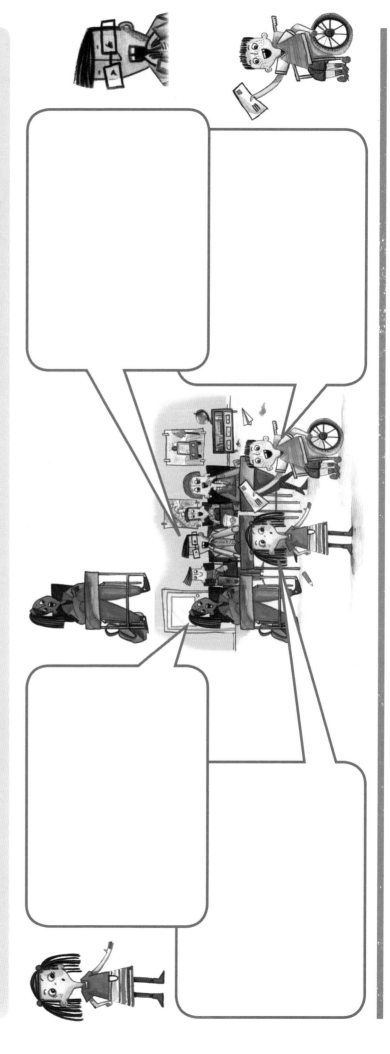

Level 10 — Pablo's Travelling Notebook

Name _____   Date _____

Read through the list of words with your partner. Find each of the words in *Pablo's Travelling Notebook*. Write down the sentence in the story where each word appears. Talk with your partner about what you think each word means. Use a dictionary to check your ideas, then write down a definition.

New word	Sentence in the story	Dictionary definition
continued (page 4)		
hiked (page 8)		
bustling (page 20)		
tumbled (page 20)		
impatiently (page 21)		

Level 10 — Pablo's Travelling Notebook

Name _____ Date _____

In *Pablo's Travelling Notebook*, Ernie the Explorer travels the world. Look at the images below, then write in the countries that Ernie visits and the things he does in each country. The last picture has been left blank for you to complete with your favourite holiday destination.

The Dog of Truth

Level 10

Name _____ Date _____

After reading *The Dog of Truth*, read the statements below. Discuss each of the statements with your partner and decide whether you agree or disagree with each one. Then cut out the statements and organize them into an Agree and a Disagree pile. Discuss your ideas with another pair.

The truth can hurt	Honesty is always best
Anyone can be part of a team	The Dog of Truth would be a good pet to have

Level 10

The Dog of Truth

Name _____ Date _____

Look through *The Dog of Truth* with your partner and find the pictures below. Talk to your partner about what the Dog of Truth is thinking at each point. Write down your ideas in the thought bubbles.

| Level 10 | **Agent Blue and the Super-smelly Goo**

Name _____ Date _____

After reading *Agent Blue and the Super-smelly Goo*, find five facts about Agent Blue and add them to your bubble map. Share your ideas with your partner.

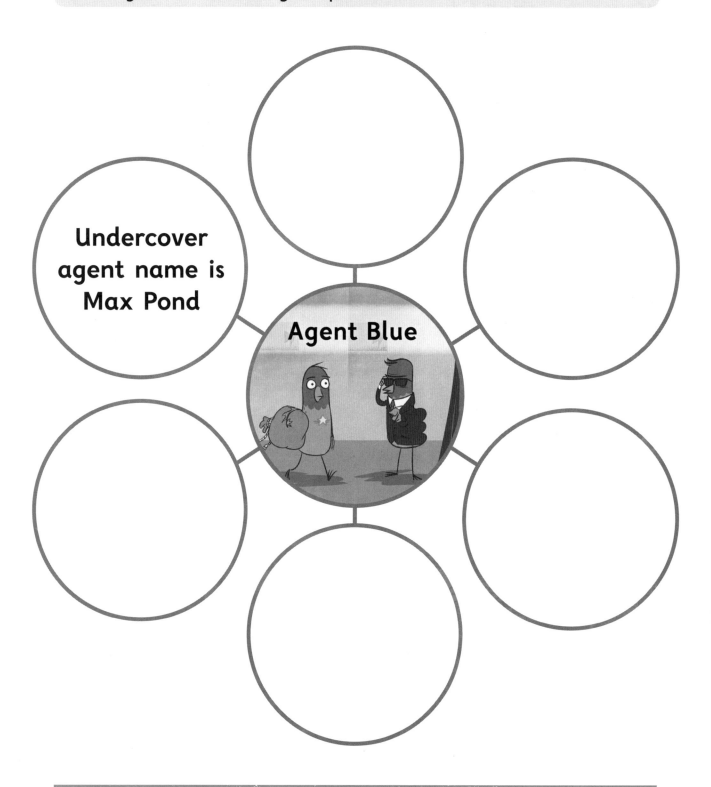

Level 10

Agent Blue and the Super-smelly Goo

Name _____ Date _____

After you have read *Agent Blue and the Super-smelly Goo*, read the questions below. Do you think the answers are in the book or not in the book? Discuss with a partner and draw a line from each question to the correct box. Now work with your partner to make up some more questions about the story. Can the answers be found in the book or not?

Answer is in the book

Answer is not in the book

How does Agent Blue train to be a spy?

Why does Birdseed want to ruin the Golden Feather Awards?

Stanley Manners

Level 11

Name _____ Date _____

Read through the list of words with your partner. Find each of the words in *Stanley Manners*. Write down the sentence in the story where each word appears. Talk with your partner about what you think each word means. Use a dictionary to check your ideas, then write down a definition.

New word	Sentence in the story	Definition
hesitantly (page 24)		
whipped (page 38)		
lumbered (page 40)		
scorching (page 41)		
colossal (page 43)		

Level 11

Stanley Manners

Name _____ Date _____

Draw pictures in the boxes below to retell the story, *Stanley Manners*. Try adding speech bubbles and captions. Use your drawings to retell the story to your partner.

I have super powers!

Stanley Manners told big lies!

Level 11

Rhyme Slime

Name _____ Date _____

After you have read *Rhyme Slime*, read the questions below. Do you think the questions have one answer or more than one answer? Discuss with a partner and draw a line from each question to the correct box. Now work with your partner to make up some more questions about the story. Do the questions have one answer or more than one answer?

Why does Dad get cross with Jasmine?

Where did the children catch Rhyme Slime from?

Question has one answer

Question has more than one answer

Level 11 # Rhyme Slime

Name _____ Date _____

> Use your knowledge of the story, *Rhyme Slime*, to work out what the missing words are. Write them in the gaps. Check your story makes sense by reading it to your partner. Have you used the same words or different ones?

Jasmine woke up feeling very _____.
By the time she got to _____ it was worse than she feared.

   There was a poem _____ inside her brain. She could not switch it off and it was a bit of a _____.

   Mrs Sprout had _____ them at the park. She said if they got slimed, they'd be _____ by dark.

_____ got cross when he thought Jasmine was pretending.
But her verses seemed never _____.

   Back in class, Miss _____ had it, too. Every child was rhyming, _____ could they do?

   Mrs Sprout came to the _____.
Never again did they _____ in pond slime and goo.

Level 11

Out of Control

Name _____ Date _____

Read through the list of words with your partner. Find each of the words in *Out of Control*. Write down the sentence in the story where each word appears. Talk with your partner about what you think the words mean. Use a dictionary to check your ideas, then write down a definition.

New word	Sentence in the story	Dictionary definition
hard (page 6, 9, 36)		
abandoned (page 11, 25)		
hesitate (page 18, 44)		
sprinted (page 31)		
shuddered (page 32)		

Level 11

Out of Control

Name _____ Date _____

In *Out of Control*, Jake and Sam are brothers. But are they alike? Discuss the two characters with your partner and identify their similarities and differences. Write your ideas in the bubbles, then share your ideas with another pair.

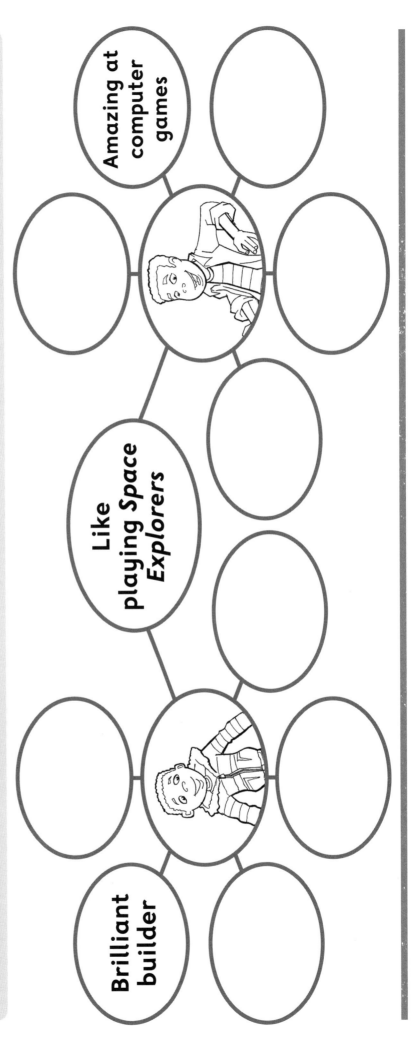

Level 11

Do Tigers Have Nine Lives?

Name _____ Date _____

Before reading *Do Tigers Have Nine Lives?*, write down everything you know about tigers in the circle below. Write where you learned this information in the rectangle. Share your ideas with your partner and add any new ideas to your diagram.

Level 11   # Do Tigers Have Nine Lives?

Name _____ Date _____

Read through the list of words with your partner. Find each of the words in *Do Tigers Have Nine Lives?* and write down the sentence in the story where each word appears. Talk with your partner about what you think each word means. Use a dictionary to check your ideas, then write down a definition.

New word	Sentence in the story	Dictionary definition
nudged (page 8)		
clambered (page 10)		
dashed (page 22)		
cries (page 24)		
deep (page 28)		

Level 11

Name _____ Date _____

Julia Caesar

Before reading *Julia Caesar*, write down everything you know about the Romans in the circle below. Write where you learned this information in the rectangle. Share your ideas with your partner and add any new ideas to your diagram.

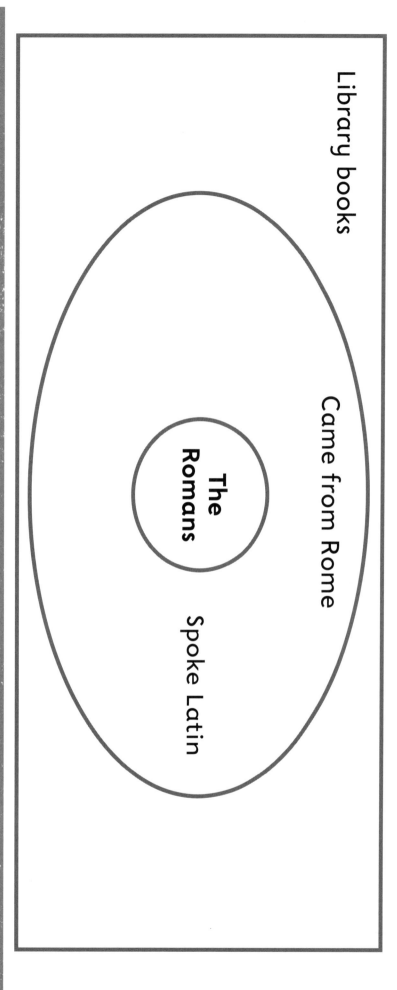

Level 11   # Julia Caesar

Name _____   Date _____

Read through the list of words with your partner. Find each of the words in *Julia Caesar*. Write down the sentence in the story where each word appears. Talk with your partner about what you think each word means. Use a dictionary to check your ideas, then write down a definition.

New word	Sentence in the story	Definition
gown (page 3, 4, 7, etc.)		
feast (page 4, 5, 14, etc.)		
powerful (page 4, 48)		
rummaging (page 38)		
distraction (page 41)		

© Oxford University Press 2015   This may be reproduced for class use within purchaser's institution

Agent Blue and the Swirly Whirly

Name _____ Date _____

Before reading Agent Blue and the Swirly Whirly, write down everything you know about secret agents in the circle below. Write where you learned this information in the rectangle. Share your ideas with your partner and add any new ideas to your diagram.

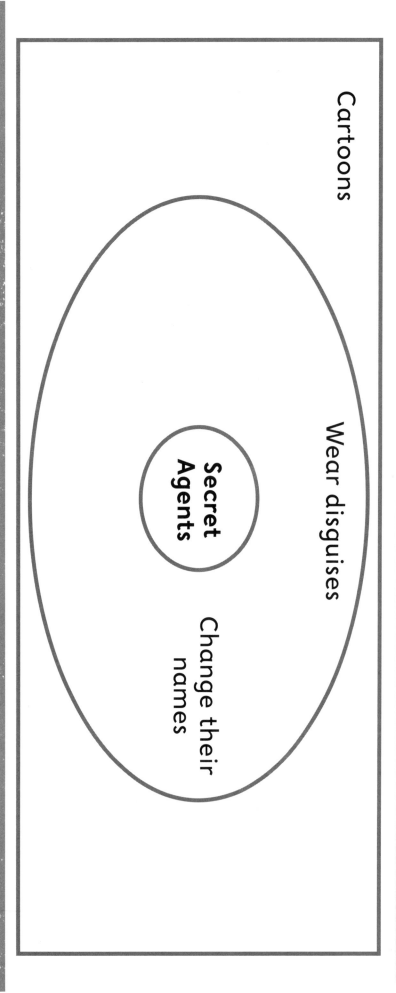

Agent Blue and the Swirly Whirly

Level 11

Name _____ Date _____

Look at page 48 in *Agent Blue and the Swirly Whirly*. This story ends with a cliffhanger. Talk to your partner about what you think might happen next. Discuss what each character might be thinking and write your ideas in the bubbles. Work in a small group and use your thought bubbles to perform a role play.

OXFORD
UNIVERSITY PRESS

Great Clarendon Street, Oxford, OX2 6DP, United Kingdom

Oxford University Press is a department of the University of Oxford.
It furthers the University's objective of excellence in research, scholarship,
and education by publishing worldwide. Oxford is a registered trade mark
of Oxford University Press in the UK and in certain other countries

Text © Oxford University Press 2015

The moral rights of the author have been asserted

First published 2015

All rights reserved. No part of this publication may
be reproduced, stored in a retrieval system, or transmitted,
in any form or by any means, without the prior permission in
writing of Oxford University Press, or as expressly permitted
by law, by licence or under terms agreed with the appropriate
reprographics rights organization. Enquiries concerning
reproduction outside the scope of the above should be sent to the
Rights Department, Oxford University Press, at the address above.

You must not circulate this work in any other form
and you must impose this same condition on any acquirer

British Library Cataloguing in Publication Data
Data available

ISBN: 978-0-19-835632-5

10 9 8 7 6 5 4 3 2 1

Paper used in the production of this book is a natural, recyclable product
made from wood grown in sustainable forests. The manufacturing process
conforms to the environmental regulations of the country of origin.

Printed in Great Britain by Ashford Colour Press

Acknowledgements

Series Advisor: Nikki Gamble

Cover illustration by Jago

Illustrations by Ros Asquith, Agnese Baruzzi, Galia Bernstein, Alicia Borges,
Kelly Canby, Andrea Castellani, Rebecca Clements, Marcus Cutler, Russ Daff,
Sergio De Giorgi, Olga Demidova, Jenni Desmond, Thomas Docherty,
Clare Elsom, Christiane Engel, Luke Flowers, Michael Garton, Anaïs Goldemberg,
Sarah Horne, Anna Hymas, Bill Ledger, Bistra Masseva, Shane McGowan,
Emi Ordás, Louise Pigott, Matt Robertson, Tony Ross, Shahab Shamshirsaz, Jago,
Zak Simmonds-Hurn, Jamie Smart, Jonatronix, Steve Stone and Ben Whitehouse